ANXIETY RELIEF BOOK FOR KIDS

Anxiety Relief Book for Kids

Activities to Understand and Overcome Worry, Fear, and Stress

EHRIN WEISS, PhD

Illustrations by Michelle Simpson

ROCKRIDGE
PRESS

This book is dedicated to all the patients who have given me the opportunity to teach them ways to handle their anxiety, and to my friends and family, who have supported me in all my efforts to become a better therapist.

Interior and Cover Designer: Michael Cook
Art Producer: Sue Bischofberger
Editors: Seth Schwartz and Nora Spiegel
Production Manager: Riley Hoffman

Illustrations © 2021 Michelle Simpson

ISBN: Print 978-1-64876-125-6 | eBook 978-1-64876-126-3

R1

CONTENTS

· ·

FOR PARENTS AND CAREGIVERS

· ·

Anxiety is a natural part of life and one of the most common mental health challenges in people of all ages. It's also one of the most treatable. This book will empower you with the knowledge and the most effective tools to help your child find freedom from anxiety, providing them (and you!) with skills you can use for the rest of your lives. Here, you'll find information and activities that are based on the most cutting-edge treatments for anxiety— cognitive behavioral therapy (CBT) and mindfulness—approaches that have strong research to support their effectiveness in the treatment of anxiety.

Encourage your child to take their time working through this book. One of the most important tools they can learn is that expressing their feelings can actually be fun, and they will have many opportunities to do that through activities like drawing and writing. Doing a little bit at a time will help your child really learn the information and get the hang of using the tools at a comfortable pace.

Doing the activities in this book may not always be easy for your child, and some ups and downs along the way are perfectly normal. When this happens, listen to your child's concerns and try to understand their perspective. Acknowledge that dealing with anxiety is a big challenge, while also gently encouraging them that they *can* do hard things.

There may also be times when you and your child need more support and guidance from a trained professional. This book can be helpful to use along with therapy, and in the More for Parents and Caregivers section I suggest some organizations where you can learn more (see page 88).

By learning the tools in this book, you are helping your child get a head start on how to handle worry and anxiety in the healthiest way possible, setting them up with the skills and confidence to face their fears—both now and in the future!

FOR KIDS

Welcome to your worry guidebook! I know it's no fun feeling nervous or scared, being shy around people, or having annoying thoughts that just won't stop, and it can be hard to know what to do to help yourself feel better. This guidebook will help you get from the land of worry and anxiety to the land of "I can handle it!"

I'm proud of you for making the decision to read this book to learn new ways to deal with worry and anxiety, and I'm excited to be your guide on this journey! Like you, I used to be a kid who worried a lot. The skills in this book are things that have helped me feel better, and now I get to help kids like you learn ways to feel better, too.

This book has lots of fun activities that will help you learn and practice different tools for dealing with worry and anxiety. Take your time working through the activities so you have a chance to see which tools work best for you. By the time you're done with this book, you'll be a worry and anxiety expert!

This journey won't always be easy. Sometimes it will feel fun and interesting, and sometimes it will feel challenging. But if you're reading this book, I bet you're up for those challenges. Learning how to handle worry and anxiety so they don't feel so scary and hard anymore is worth the effort.

Are you ready? Let's get started!

CHAPTER 1

WHAT ARE MY WORRIES?

Do you ever wonder if worries are normal? Or what worries even are? The first step in learning how to handle worries is to understand them. Understanding what worries are, and knowing what *your* worries are, will help you recognize worry when it's happening. When you can recognize worry, you'll be able to know when it's time to use the skills you learn later in this book.

In this chapter, you'll learn about different kinds of worries, and you'll get to do some activities to help you get to know your own worries better.

WHAT ARE WORRIES?

If you're reading this book, you might be a kid who worries a lot. Maybe you've even been told, "You worry too much!" But what *exactly* are worries? A worry is a type of thought. Worry thoughts are usually about something bad happening that hasn't happened yet, and might not ever happen, but that you think *could* happen. Maybe you even think it WILL happen. A lot of times, worry thoughts start with "What if . . . ?"

What if I get sick?
What if I fail that test?
What if people laugh at me?

A lot of kids worry about things like getting hurt, making mistakes, or people getting mad at them. Worries can be about any bad thing you think could happen. These types of thoughts make people feel anxious, nervous, or scared.

Even though worries often start with "what if," the question isn't what kids are really worried about. It's the answer to the "what if?" question that makes them feel anxious. And our imaginations sure can come up with all kinds of scary answers that can seem very convincing. Even though they really come from your brain, it can feel like worries have a mind of their own.

It can actually help to think of worries as coming from outside of you. Some people like to compare worries to a bug, buzzing around their heads like a pest that just won't go away. Some people think about worries like they're a scary noise coming from behind a closed door—they may feel afraid of what's on the other side, but when they are brave enough to open the door, they see it was just a trick and there was nothing to be afraid of after all. As you work through this book, you'll see that most of the time, things don't turn out nearly as bad as worries tell you they will.

Here's another way to think about worries. Have you ever known someone who exaggerated things a lot? Maybe they told you something easy to

believe, like they had a birthday party, but then added details that made it hard to believe, like they had a thousand guests and a hundred-foot-tall cake that everyone climbed before taking rides on a real-life unicorn.

A friend like this might try really hard to convince you that their stories are true, and even get mad at you for not believing them. They might even try to get you to make decisions based on their false information.

If this friend seemed to care about you, and was even helpful at times, you might want to keep them around. But would you trust everything they told you, knowing they exaggerated so much? Do you think you would believe everything this friend said?

Probably not. You'd probably want to do some investigating yourself before deciding which things to believe (like they had a party with guests and cake and had fun) and which things to ignore (that there were a thousand guests, a cake so big people could climb it, and a mythical creature at the party).

Worry is a lot like this friend. Sometimes it seems to want what's best for you and may even give you helpful or important information, but it exaggerates A LOT. You might even want to give your worry friend a name, like "Worrying Wally," or "Exaggerating Edna."

Sometimes kids know what their worry thoughts are, and sometimes their worry is more like a feeling, like being scared or nervous or just really not wanting to do something. If you're one of those kids who feels scared a lot but you don't know why, it's okay. The exercises in this book can help you figure out what's really bothering you. It might be hard to think about sometimes, but I know you can do it!

WHAT COULD THE WORRY BE?

If you're not sure what you're feeling worried about, it can help to think of what another kid might feel worried about.

Fill in the thought bubble. What do you think this kid is feeling scared, nervous, or anxious about? You can draw or write your answer.

Is this something you feel scared, nervous, or anxious about, too?

WHAT ARE MY "WHAT IFS"?

Remember earlier when we talked about "what ifs" and how it's the answer to this question that really makes worries feel scary? In this activity, you'll get to know your own "what ifs" better.

First, write down one of your "what if" thoughts, then write the answer that worries you: What do you think will happen? Or what's the worst thing that could happen? Keep answering, "What if that happens?" for each new thought until you're out of answers. Worries often have lots of layers, and this exercise will help you get to the bottom of what you are worried about.

Example:

What if I didn't study enough? Then I'll fail the test.

And what if that happens? Then I'll get a bad grade in the class.

And what if that happens? Then I'll fail the class.

And what if that happens? Then I'll have to repeat the grade and I won't have any friends.

Now, it's your turn!

What if _____

_____?

Then (fill in your worry)_____

_____.

And what if that happens?

Then (fill in your answer) _____

_____.

And what if that happens?

Then (now answer that "what if")_____

_____.

    This exercise can bring up a lot of emotions, and if you're feeling a little overwhelmed right now, that's totally normal. But guess what? You just identified one of your worst fears! This is actually a huge step in figuring out how to cope with them, which we are going to explore later in this book. Diving deep into your worries like this takes a lot of courage. Keep up the good work!

ARE WORRIES NORMAL?

If you're a kid who worries a lot, you might feel like you're the only one who worries and that worrying so much means there's something wrong with you. This can feel scary or embarrassing, and can become another thing for you to worry about.

    But I have good news for you! Ready? Everybody feels scared or worried sometimes. Worrying a lot is pretty common for kids *and* grown-ups. In fact, worrying can be a good thing!

    How can this be? Did you know that all emotions—even the ones that don't feel good—give you important information? Remember that worrying is thinking about things that could go wrong that haven't yet. Even though it can make you feel scared or anxious, worrying can help protect you or prepare you for those things.

    Think for a minute about what would happen if you, or other people, never worried. You might be more likely to say or do something that you would regret later, like being mean to people, not following rules, or doing dangerous things. Sometimes worrying can help you make better choices and be ready for things that could happen.

    If worry can be so good, why does it feel so bad? That bad feeling is like a warning to get your attention. People don't like feeling bad, so they will usually try to find ways to feel better. If worry didn't make you feel bad, you might just ignore it!

For example, if you worry that people won't like you and will think you're mean, you might be more likely to say something nice (like giving a compliment) and keep unkind thoughts to yourself. Worrying about getting bad grades may make you more likely to study so that you know the material. So, even though you might wish you could get rid of all your worries, that probably wouldn't be a very good idea. Having just the right amount of worry and even fear can be helpful.

But just like getting rid of all your worry could cause problems, having too much worry can cause problems, too. This can happen when worries get too big, happen too often, or last too long. Remember in the last section when we talked about how worries can be like a friend who exaggerates a lot? Imagine if that friend  told you, "Hey, you could fall and get hurt on the monkey bars. They're really hard, and you're not very strong. You should stay away."

If you completely ignored this friend and went for the highest rung and tried to do tricks like hanging upside down without testing your strength, you might fall and get hurt. Listening shows you care about your safety and want to be responsible.

But if you believed everything this voice said, you might feel too anxious to find out how strong you really are! You might even feel too anxious to try other playground equipment. These would be signs that worry has gone from being helpful to harmful and interfering with your life.

When this happens, it can make you want to stop doing things you used to enjoy, want to try, or need to do. Or it can make those things a lot harder and less enjoyable. It can get in the way of friendships. It can feel frustrating for both kids and parents, and sometimes it can lead to arguments. This is why it's important to be able to recognize the ways worry is good and helpful, and the ways it is hurtful and causes problems. This will help you keep the good parts of worry and learn to say, "I don't think so, Anxious Andy!" to the exaggerated parts.

WHAT'S GOOD ABOUT MY WORRIES?

Now let's figure out what's good about *your* worries. Think about the worries you wrote about in other activities. Get out a pencil and circle the following statements that are good things about your worries.

I care about other people's feelings　**I'm more organized**

I want to do my best　**I follow rules**

I love my family　**I keep things clean**

I care about my future　**I make sure to be prepared**

I'm responsible　**I want people to like me**

I don't want to get hurt　**I want to be safe**

I'm more careful

Now add your own!

What do my worries show I care about?

_____

_____

_____

How are my worries trying to help me?

_____

_____

_____

WHAT PROBLEMS DO MY WORRIES CAUSE?

Great job at coming up with ways that your worries can actually be helpful, and the good things those worries show about you! I hope you can see how worry really can be like a friend. But remember, this is a friend who also exaggerates . . . a lot!

Write or draw about two or three problems of yours that were caused by listening to worry's exaggerations, or things these exaggerations have kept you from doing.

MY FAVORITE PART

In this chapter, you learned:

- Worries can be like a friend who exaggerates a lot.

- Worry is normal—everyone worries sometimes.

- Worry can be helpful and show good things about you.

- Worry becomes a problem when it gets in the way of living your life.

You also had the chance to:

- Figure out what your worry thoughts are.

- Find good things about your worries and anxiety.

- Notice when worries and anxiety have gotten in the way and caused problems for you.

What was your favorite thing you learned in this chapter? What did you like about that part?

_____

_____

_____

_____

_____

★ **CHAPTER 2** ★

WHY DO I WORRY SO MUCH?

Now you know more about what worry is, and how important it is to be able to worry and feel anxious *some* of the time. You also have a pretty good idea of what your worries are, and what can be good about your worries.

In this chapter, you'll learn even more about worry, like where your worries come from, what makes your worry alarm go off, and the emotions and physical sensations your worries bring up. The more you know about worries and understand *your* worries, the less bad and scary they will feel. This will also help you feel ready to do the worry-busting activities later in this book!

WHERE DO MY WORRIES COME FROM?

Even though worry can be normal and helpful, it sure doesn't feel good sometimes. You may wonder why you have these problems when other kids don't seem to. You might never know *exactly* where your anxiety comes from. But this chapter will give you some ideas.

Do any of your family members feel anxious a lot? People don't always say when they're feeling worried or anxious, but sometimes you can tell by how they act, if you pay close attention. Maybe you have a parent who is always asking you if you're really sure you've done all your homework (even though you always do), or an aunt or uncle who cleans a lot or is always double-checking to make sure they turned off the stove and locked all the doors, or a grandparent who is afraid to fly. One thing we know is that anxiety often runs in families. This means that if one person in a family has anxiety or worries a lot, they are more likely to have relatives who also feel that way.

Another possible reason some kids might worry more than others is that there can be differences in the brains and bodies of people who get anxious easily. They might be more sensitive to small changes in how their bodies feel (kind of like a smoke alarm that goes off every time someone cooks food instead of only when there's a fire), and it might take their bodies longer to calm down and get back to their normal level.

Sometimes there are outside forces that can make a kid feel more worried or anxious. For example, they might see other people acting scared or anxious about things and can learn to be afraid of those things, too. Or they might have something stressful happen, like moving or their parents divorcing or other big life changes, or they might feel pressure to do a lot of things or perform well.

Some kids start to feel anxious a lot after something happens to them that feels really bad or scary. Getting sick or hurt, being in an accident or really bad storm, being treated unfairly, or having someone you love get hurt or die are examples of things that can be really upsetting. Some kids worry about those things happening again, which can make them feel anxious anytime something reminds them of that scary event.

There are even times when kids really feel some other feeling, but they don't realize it, and instead they feel anxious. This is called a hidden emotion. It happens when something is bothering you that you think you should be okay with, so you hide the fact that it's bothering you from everyone—even yourself! This happens a lot to kids who are really nice and don't want to upset anyone, so their brains hide their real feelings and they only realize they feel anxious. For example, you might feel angry when your parents bug you about practicing piano all the time, but you think you should be okay with it, so instead you feel anxious about upsetting your parents.

As you can see, there are a lot of places that worry can come from, and the answer can be different for everyone. It may be that your worry comes from one or a combination of several of these things, or even someplace else. It may feel helpful to have an idea of where your worry or anxiety comes from, but it's okay if you don't know exactly what's causing it; you can still learn to feel better!

FLIP THE SCRIPT

You've been answering a lot of questions. Do you want to take a turn asking them? Learning about other people's experiences can help you understand yourself better (and remind you that you're not alone!). Find a friend or a parent or other relative who would be willing to answer some questions for you about worry or anxiety. Ask the questions one at a time and write down their answers.

These interview questions will get you started. Feel free to add your own!

1. When are some times you've felt worried or anxious?

_____

_____

2. Do you ever think you worry or feel anxious too much?

_____

_____

3. Have your worries ever been wrong or exaggerated?

_____

_____

4. Fill in your own question: _____?

_____

_____

MY IDEAS . . . WHERE MIGHT MY ANXIETY COME FROM?

Now that you know some of the places worry and anxiety can come from, think about where *your* worry and anxiety could be coming from. Each of the following boxes has a question to help you think about the different parts of where your anxiety and worry could be coming from.

Get out a pencil or something colorful to write with and write or draw your answers in the boxes.

Have any of my family members felt anxious or worried a lot?	Are there ways my body is more sensitive to changes or slower to calm down?
Are there situations that have happened or are still happening in my life that make me feel more scared or anxious?	Are there any other things bothering me at times when I feel worried or anxious?

WHY DOES MY ALARM GO OFF?

Do you remember in the last chapter when I said worry could be like a warning to get your attention? People sometimes say that anxiety is like an alarm going off. Another name for this is the "fight-flight-freeze response." It's what happens in your brain and your body when you feel threatened or like you're in danger.

A helpful way of understanding this can be to imagine you're going for a walk in the woods and you run into a bear. How scary! You'll need to figure out how to protect yourself, and fast! This usually means trying to fight the bear or run away. Or you might freeze first while you figure out what to do and get your body prepared for action. Your body was designed to realize there's a threat and prepare to protect yourself quickly.

This fight-flight-freeze response is controlled by networks in your brain that we can think of as the "fear center" of your brain. This part becomes aware of threats before the thinking parts of your brain do, and it sounds the alarm, sending information up into the thinking parts of your brain and down into your body to tell them to react.

You can think of this part as being kind of like a crossing guard in your brain (page 12). Some people have a crossing guard that does a pretty good job of deciding when it's safe to cross and when it's time to stay on the side of the road. If there's a danger, their crossing guard quickly tells them they're in danger. If the coast is clear, it lets them cross. When the threat part of your brain is working like it's meant to, it protects you from real danger and takes a break when the coast is clear.

If you feel anxious or worried a lot, it could be that this part of your brain is extra sensitive, kind of like that smoke alarm we talked about in the last section that goes off whenever someone's cooking food. You can think of this as having a crossing guard who takes their job a little too seriously. Your crossing guard may be extra cautious, telling you it's dangerous to cross even when there's nothing coming. They might hear a noise far in the distance and tell you not to cross *just in case* a car is coming. If you try to cross anyway, they might yell and try to stop you. But if you listen to them, you'll be stuck on the corner, not able to get where you want to go! This is like a false alarm.

Most of us aren't living in the forest and running into bears much. Most of the time, the threats you're perceiving and things you feel afraid of, like people getting mad at you, making mistakes, or getting sick, are not real life-or-death situations. But they can still feel like they are, and our bodies can still react like our lives depend on it. This can make you feel like you need to do something extreme to make sure you'll be okay when you're in a situation that you feel worried or anxious about.

It makes sense that you would feel that way when worry is exaggerating and making your body's alarm bells go off. If you're a kid who has a lot of false alarms, part of your job will be to teach your extra-careful crossing guard that it doesn't need to be so cautious to keep you safe—that it doesn't need to sound the alarm for every small change in your body or surroundings, and that the risk of danger isn't as high as it thinks. An alarm doesn't always mean there's real danger. The tools in this book will help you learn that.

TRUE ALARM OR FALSE ALARM?

If you're going to retrain your crossing guard, you'll need to be able to help it tell the difference between "true alarms" (times when there's real danger) and "false alarms" (times when we worry, but nothing bad happens).

Let's practice! For each kid in the following paragraphs, is their anxiety a true alarm or a false alarm? Circle your answer.

1. Marco and his friends were playing soccer and their ball rolled into a busy road. Marco stopped when he got to the curb and waited for traffic to stop before he ran into the street for the ball. **True alarm** or **false alarm**?

2. Sam threw up in school one day. He's afraid it will happen again, and asks to stay home from school several times a week because his stomach hurts. If he finds out someone else has been sick, he stays far away from them. **True alarm** or **false alarm**?

3. If Jenna gets a B on any assignment, she feels very anxious. She worries that she won't be able to get into a good high school or college or get a good job if she doesn't get all A's. Any time she has to turn in an assignment, she worries that she'll get a bad grade. **True alarm** or **false alarm**?

4. Kishi saw a car crash right in front of his father's car, and his father had to swerve to avoid crashing, too. Kishi felt scared. He was worried they could crash. **True alarm** or **false alarm**?

(**Key:** 1 – T, 2 – F, 3 – F, 4 – T)

MY FALSE ALARMS

Think of all the times you can remember when your alarm went off, but your worry didn't come true. Noticing when this happens can help your crossing guard learn when it's overreacting and help you learn when the alarms are probably false. It can even help train your crossing guard to have more appropriate responses in the future! Write down as many times as you can remember to make a "False Alarm" list.

What I was afraid would happen that didn't happen:

1. _____

2. _____

3. _____

4. _____

5. _____

6. _____

7. _____

8. _____

9. _____

10. _____

MY FAVORITE PART

In this chapter, you learned:

- We usually don't know exactly where all our worries come from or why we worry so much, and that's okay!

- The fight-flight-freeze response is our body's way of protecting us when there's danger.

- The "fear center" of our brain is like a crossing guard that tells us when there's danger.

- People who feel anxious or scared a lot might have an overactive part of the brain that causes many false alarms.

You also had the chance to:

- Think about where your anxiety and worry might come from.

- Learn more about other people's experiences with anxiety and worry.

- Practice telling the difference between true alarms and false alarms.

- Think about times when you've had false alarms.

What was your favorite thing you learned in this chapter. What did you like about that part?

_____

_____

_____

_____

CHAPTER 3

WHAT DOES WORRYING FEEL LIKE?

Do you feel like you understand worry better now? Hopefully it doesn't feel so mysterious anymore. You've learned a lot! Now you might be thinking, "Okay, I understand what worry is and I have an idea about why it happens. But is this what a worry *feels* like?" If your feelings still seem confusing, or if you have a lot of questions about how you feel when you worry, this chapter is for you! In this chapter, you'll learn more about feelings—both the emotions and the physical sensations worries bring up—and why worry feels the way it does.

WHAT ARE FEELINGS?

When you talk about feelings, you probably think of words like happy, sad, mad, or scared. Another word for feelings is *emotions*. These are words we use to describe how our bodies are feeling on the inside. Some emotions feel good to have, and some don't feel very good, but all feelings are okay, and everybody has them.

You might want to ignore unpleasant feelings or just make them go away. But all feelings are important! Even feelings that are difficult and uncomfortable help us understand ourselves and what we need.

You've already learned about how worrying and feeling anxious can be good because they can help protect you and show good things about you. Well, that's true for all feelings; all feelings can show something good about you and be helpful in some way. When you understand yourself and your feelings, you can make better choices so you can get along with others better and enjoy your life more.

Being able to name your feelings with words is an important step. When you know how you're feeling, it's easier to tell others how you feel. If you're having a feeling you don't like, knowing how you feel can help you figure out how to feel better— or help other people figure out how to help you. Even just naming how you're feeling can help you feel better. When we are able to name our difficult feelings, they lose some of their power.

Did you know you can have more than one feeling at a time? In fact, people usually have several feelings at once. Sometimes they know what all their feelings are, and sometimes they don't. A lot of times, kids who feel anxious also feel mad or sad or scared. Sometimes the anxious or scared feelings are the ones that they are more aware of, or sometimes they notice and show the mad or sad feelings more.

Even feelings that don't seem to fit together can happen at the same time. For example, you can feel happy and sad or excited and nervous at the same time. We call this having mixed feelings. Mixed feelings can be confusing, but they're normal, too. Just remember, all feelings are giving you information. And you get to be the detective who figures out what they're trying to tell you!

It's also good to know that different people can have different feelings about the same situation. This doesn't mean that one of you is right and the other is wrong. Both of you probably have good reasons for feeling the way you do. Can you think of a time you and another person had different feelings about something?

I like to think of feelings as being like emotional weather. Just like the weather is sometimes sunny, warm, stormy, cloudy, cold, or some combination of these (you can even have sunny storms!), our feelings are sometimes happy, sad, mad, scared, or some combination of these feelings or others. And just like the weather can change and all types of weather can be helpful at times, feelings also change, and all feelings help us in some ways at times. When you're having a feeling that's uncomfortable, it can help to remember that, like weather, feelings don't last forever.

GETTING TO KNOW MY FEELINGS BETTER

Now pick a feeling you have a lot and do the following activity. It will help you recognize when you and other people are experiencing this feeling.

Feeling: _____

Write about a time you felt this way.

_____

_____

_____

How does your body feel when you're having this feeling?

_____

_____

How can other people tell you're feeling this way? What do you say or do?

_____

_____

Now you and a grown-up act it out! Think about a time you felt this way, try to bring those feelings into your body, and show what it looks like. You can take turns acting it out or do it together.

NOTICING AND UNDERSTANDING MIXED FEELINGS

Draw about a time when you had more than one feeling at the same time.

Which feelings did you have? What was each of them trying to tell you?

_____

_____

_____

WHY DO I FEEL THIS WAY WHEN I WORRY?

Do you remember when we talked about how worries are thoughts that can make you feel nervous, anxious, or scared? Some people think this means that anxiety is all in their heads. But it's not! Whether it's a worry thought or something outside of us that sets off our danger alarm, it causes real physical changes in our bodies.

There are two types of feelings we can talk about with worry: our sensations, or the way our bodies feel inside, and our emotions, which are the words we use to describe those feelings.

In the moment when your alarm goes off, you might feel nervous, anxious, scared, or panicky. You might even feel angry or numb. Over time, if you don't learn ways to deal with these feelings and they keep happening again and again, it can get harder to feel happy, and you might start to feel bad about yourself, or get grumpy a lot. These are all common emotions that happen with worry. But why do they happen?

To understand this, it can be helpful to know what physical changes happen in our bodies when we worry, and why those happen. Remember, the fight-flight-freeze response is our body's way of preparing to protect itself from possible danger. Imagine you were in a building and the fire alarm went off. Right away, your body's own alarm response would take over, and you'd try to figure out how to leave the building or put out the fire. Your body would prepare for action.

In the moment when your fight-flight-freeze response takes over, your body makes a lot of changes to prepare for action. Freezing usually comes first when you're surprised by something that feels scary or threatening. You might feel like your muscles tense up and everything in your body stops— like your body steps on the brakes instead of the gas. When this happens, it's your body's way of stopping to figure out what's happening and how to react. Some people freeze for longer than others, and you might freeze for longer in some situations than others.

After you freeze, you might notice that your heart starts to beat really hard, or that your breath gets faster. These changes help get energy to your arms and legs so they can help you fight or run. The brakes are off, and it's time for action! Those tense muscles and changes in where your blood is flowing can make some people feel jittery, shaky, sweaty, cold, or hot. These changes might also make you feel a little dizzy or have trouble focusing. Some people also notice that their mouth feels really dry, or their stomach hurts or feels fluttery. When worry happens too often or lasts too long, these physical sensations may happen more regularly, in addition to physical aches and pains and trouble sleeping.

When your body feels this way, it can be confusing and scary, especially if you aren't sure why it's happening. Just having these feelings can make it seem like something is definitely wrong, and that you need to stay on high alert to be ready for whatever might happen.

Knowing that these are signs of anxiety, and that it could be a false alarm, can help make these experiences feel less scary and confusing, and can be a step toward feeling better!

WHEN DOES MY BODY FEEL WORRIED?

Write or draw about a time you were feeling worried.

WHERE DO I FEEL MY WORRIES?

Write or draw your physical sensations on the following picture where they happen on your body. Here's a list of ideas to get you started, but you can add your own:

- Heart beating fast or hard

- Upset stomach

- Sweating

- Headache

- Stomachache

- Butterflies in stomach

- Tense muscles

- Shaking

- Sweating

- Trouble focusing

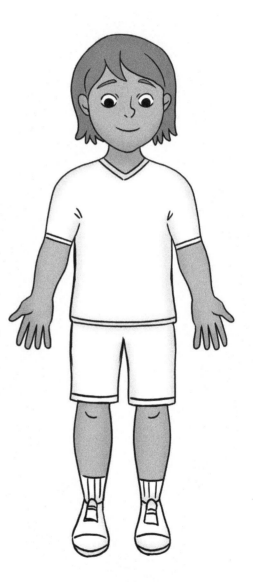

MY FAVORITE PART

In this chapter, you learned:

- Feelings give us important information.

- All feelings are okay, even if they don't feel good.

- Feelings are like emotional weather: they don't last forever.

- The sensations you feel when you're worried help your body protect itself from possible danger.

You also had the chance to:

- Practice recognizing your feelings.

- Think about what your feelings are trying to tell you.

- Notice what happens in your body when you're worried.

- Think about times you had the physical sensations of worry and what was going on.

What was your favorite thing you learned or did in this chapter? What did you like about that part?

_____

_____

_____

_____

_____

CHAPTER 4

WHAT CAN I DO ABOUT MY WORRY THOUGHTS?

You've learned a lot about how worry exaggerates and creates false alarms, and you're probably getting the hang of starting to notice when you're having a false alarm because of worry's exaggerations. You might even be starting to question whether worry is telling you the truth. Maybe you even believe your worry less often. You're making great progress!

Even if you believe your worry less often, it's probably still pretty convincing sometimes. In this chapter, you'll learn more about how worry thoughts work and what you can do about them.

HOW DO WORRY THOUGHTS WORK?

Do you remember how we learned that different people can have different feelings about the same situation? Do you have any ideas about why this happens?

Let's look at an example and see if you can find any clues.

How do you think each of these kids is feeling? They're all on the same roller coaster, right? So it can't be the roller coaster that's causing their feelings, or they'd all feel the same way. What's different? That's right—their thoughts! It's our thoughts about a situation that cause our feelings.

Now let's take it one step further: How do you think each of these kids is going to act? Will they all act the same? Probably not. Their thoughts and feelings will lead each of them to want to act in different ways. When they get off the roller coaster, the kid who feels happy might want to ride the roller coaster again, the kid who feels sad might want to sit and cry or go home, the kid who feels mad might race to get in the front next time, and the kid who feels scared might never want to ride a roller coaster again!

This example shows how our thoughts, feelings, and actions are all connected. It can help to think of them as being like points on a triangle.

The good news is that because thoughts, feelings, and actions are all connected, if you can change even one of these things—how you're thinking, feeling, or acting—the other two will also change! Later in this chapter, we'll talk about what to do with your worry thoughts, and we'll talk about what you can do about your actions and sensations in other chapters.

But first, let's talk a little more about what happens to our thoughts when we worry. We know from the last chapter that our bodies go into survival mode (fight, flight, or freeze) when we feel scared or anxious, and that the changes this causes in our bodies can make it harder to focus on anything except for keeping ourselves safe. It's almost like there's a switch that turns off the parts of our brain that can think clearly and make the most helpful decisions.

Even if you're not in any real danger, once your alarm goes off, it can feel like you need to keep focusing on the worry thought, so you'll be prepared just in case the worry comes true. It can be hard to decide to focus on other things, because you might believe it's dangerous to stop thinking about the worry thought. Sometimes it even feels impossible! This can get in the way of doing schoolwork, learning, and having fun.

Even though this is how our brains are made to work, it's possible to get those thinking parts of your brain thinking clearly again. Learning how to flip that switch back is one of the things you can do to help yourself feel better, and we're going to learn all about that later in this book. Stay tuned!

WHICH THOUGHTS, FEELINGS, AND ACTIONS GO TOGETHER?

Jordan saw a friend, Kwame, at the store, but Kwame didn't say, "Hi." Here are some different thoughts, feelings, and actions that Jordan could have. Draw lines to connect the thoughts, feelings, and actions that go together.

THOUGHT	FEELING	ACTION
"What if Kwame's mad at me? Did I do something wrong?"	Sad	Cry
"How rude! I guess we're not friends."	Concerned	Ignore Kwame next time
"Maybe Kwame didn't see me."	Anxious	Ask if Kwame's okay
"I hope Kwame's okay! I wonder if something happened?"	Mad	Try to figure out if Kwame is mad
"I'm losing my only friend."	Fine	Act normal with Kwame

Which of these do you think would be the most helpful thought about what was going on? Why? Do you have any other ideas about how Jordan could think, feel, or act in this situation?

_____

_____

_____

MY WORRY THOUGHTS

Write your worry thoughts in the following boxes, then fill in your feelings and your actions that happen when you have these thoughts.

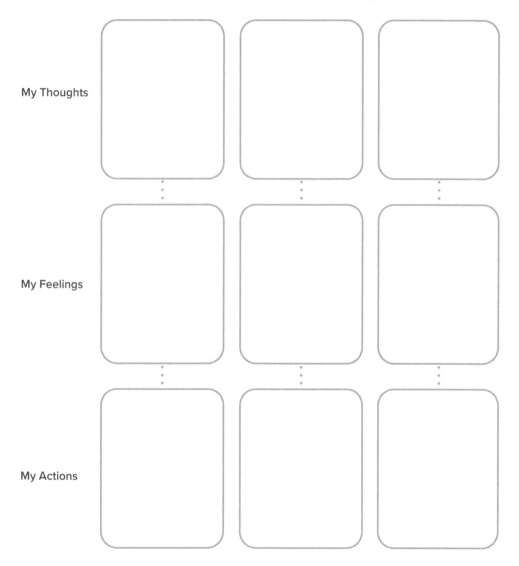

My Thoughts

My Feelings

My Actions

WHAT CAN I DO ABOUT MY WORRY THOUGHTS?

Now that you can recognize worry thoughts and how they can impact your feelings and actions, what can you do about them?

First, try really hard not to think of a penguin wearing a hat and sunglasses driving a car.

What are you thinking about right now? I bet it's a penguin driving a car, isn't it?

See, you can't just *stop* thoughts. In fact, trying to stop any thought just makes you think about it even more.

Is there anything bad or wrong about thinking of a penguin driving a car? No! The only reason it would bother you at all is that you think you *shouldn't* be thinking about it, because I told you not to. The thought isn't the problem—what you're telling yourself about the thought is the problem. (You can stop trying not to think about that penguin now, by the way.)

Obviously, some thoughts are more upsetting to think about than animals wearing clothes and driving cars. But thinking that you shouldn't have a thought makes it feel more upsetting, which can make you try harder not to have it, which can make it happen more, which then makes you more upset. Can you see the problem?

Now think about lifting your arm. Now think about screaming. Now pick up a glass of water and think about throwing it. Did you lift your arm, scream, or throw the water? Why not? Now, think about a piano crashing through your roof. Did it happen? Why not?

I bet you said, "Because just thinking about something doesn't make it happen." Bingo!

This brings us to our next important point. Ready? Here it is: Worry thoughts aren't dangerous. They're just thoughts. Remember, having a thought doesn't make it true. Our brains are thought-making machines. They're constantly thinking. That's their job! Sometimes we know what the thoughts are, and sometimes we don't. But they're always happening, and we can't just stop ourselves from having them.

What we can do is learn to recognize them and decide whether or not to believe them, and whether or not to act on them. We all have thoughts that

our brains just have on their own and thoughts that we choose to have. Just remember that what you tell yourself about your worry thoughts is more important than what the worry thoughts try to tell you.

Now take a look above at this picture of two kids taking an exam.

Both of these kids have the same worry thought ("I'm going to fail and it's going to be terrible!"), but they are telling themselves different things about that worry thought. Notice that the kid on the right doesn't try to convince herself that she will get a good grade. Instead, she reminds herself that she can handle whatever happens, even if it isn't what she wants, and that it won't be the end of the world.

To talk back to worry thoughts, it's important to figure out how the worry is exaggerating, and talk back to the exaggerated part. Try asking yourself these questions:

1. What's my worry thought? What is the worry telling me is going to happen?

2. What proof do I have that the worry is true?

3. What proof do I have that the worry is not true?

4. What else could be going on?

5. What are the chances the worry will come true?

6. If it did come true, could I handle it? What could help me handle it?

7. What's probably going to happen?

The answers to these questions will help you come up with new thoughts to tell yourself instead of believing the worry thoughts. Then you can say, "Thanks, Exaggerating Edna, but I know you're exaggerating. Here's what I think is really happening . . . "

CIRCLE GAME: IDENTIFY HELPFUL AND UNHELPFUL THOUGHTS

Now it's your turn to be a thought detective and find the thoughts that would be helpful to tell yourself.

Circle the helpful thoughts and put a big X through the unhelpful thoughts.

TALKING BACK TO MY WORRY THOUGHTS

Now it's time to practice what you've learned on your own worry thoughts. Answer the following questions using one of your worry thoughts to help you come up with a more helpful thought you can tell yourself. You can use this exercise any time you have a worry thought!

My worry thought:

_____

_____

What proof do I have that the worry is true?

_____

_____

What proof do I have that the worry is not true?

_____

_____

What else could be going on?

_____

_____

What are the chances the worry will come true?

_____

_____

If it did come true, could I handle it? What could help me handle it?

_____

_____

What can I tell myself about that worry?

_____

_____

MY FAVORITE PART

In this chapter, you learned:

- Our thoughts, feelings, and actions are all connected.

- If we can change what we're thinking or how we're acting, we can change how we're feeling.

- Worry thoughts can make it hard to focus on other things.

- Trying to stop thoughts makes those thoughts happen more.

- Thoughts are not dangerous.

- You can come up with new and more helpful thoughts, instead of believing worry thoughts.

You also had the chance to:

- See how thoughts, feelings, and actions are connected.

- Recognize helpful and unhelpful thoughts.

- Practice coming up with more helpful thoughts.

What was your favorite thing you learned or did in this chapter? What did you like about that part?

_____

_____

_____

_____

CHAPTER 5

WHY WON'T MY WORRIES JUST GO AWAY?

By now you know what worries are, and you're probably starting to understand your worries a little better. You may even be able to talk back to some of your worries. You're doing a great job! Talking back to worries can help a lot, but sometimes worries still keep coming back. If that's happening to you, you might feel frustrated or disappointed, and that's totally normal. In this chapter, you'll learn why that happens, and what you can do about it.

WHAT IF THE DOG BITES ME? (AND OTHER SITUATIONS)

Imagine you are afraid of dogs. A lot of people are afraid of dogs, so you might not even have to imagine! If you're afraid of dogs, you might be worried that the dog will bite you, jump up on you, lick you, or bark really loud. Can you think of any other reasons someone might have for feeling scared of dogs?

Most of those worries are things that really could happen with at least some dogs, and some of those things could actually be dangerous (like biting). Even the worries that are not really dangerous—like barking really loud—can still feel scary, which doesn't feel good.

If you were afraid of dogs, you'd probably be able to imagine all kinds of scary things that could happen with dogs in all kinds of different situations. A lot of times, kids who feel anxious a lot have really creative ideas and excellent imaginations. If you're a kid with a great imagination, I bet that's something you wouldn't want to change. I wouldn't want you to change that, either!

The challenge is that having a great imagination can also mean that you can imagine more possibilities of things going wrong, and our brains don't do a very good job of telling the difference between things that have actually happened and things that we've just *imagined* happening. That means you might have to do

extra work to help your brain learn when you're really in danger and when you're not.

Remember that "fear center" of your brain we talked about before? Whether you are really in danger, imagining the possibility of danger, or afraid of feeling scared, that part of your brain makes connections between your fears of and reminders of those fears. Some people call these reminders "triggers." They're kind of like magnets your fears stick to, making you feel scared or anxious anytime you're around one of those reminders.

If you were afraid of dogs, what reminders might make you feel scared? Probably seeing a dog up close, and maybe even seeing one from far away. Maybe going on walks or going to the park, riding your bike on a street where you know dogs live, or hearing a dog bark. Sometimes even seeing dogs on TV, in movies, or in pictures, or seeing or hearing the word "dog" could feel scary. You might even feel scared if you hear a song that was playing when you saw a dog!

Why do you feel scared even when you're just reminded of your fears? Remember that your fears and worries have the important job of helping you stay safe. If all dogs were really a danger to you, it wouldn't be enough to just run away when you saw a dog . . . you would need to be prepared for any situations where there might be dogs. This means you would need to know where you might be most likely to be around a dog, and be on the lookout for reminders of dogs, to keep yourself safe.

Because staying safe is one of the most important things you do, your brain is sensitive to reminders of things that could be dangerous or scary. And kids who feel worried or scared a lot have an extra-sensitive fear center, or an extra-strong reminder-collecting magnet. That means more reminders to feel scared of.

Luckily, not all dogs are dangerous! That's probably true for a lot of your fears and reminders, too. Knowing what you're afraid of, and what reminders your magnet has collected, are important steps in learning to feel better.

WHAT ARE MY REMINDERS?

Knowing what things remind you of your fears can be just as important as knowing what your fears and worries are. Pick a fear for each of the boxes below. Write the fear on the line and write or draw all the reminders you're afraid of in the box.

Fear: _____

Fear: _____

WHAT COULD MAKE MY FEARS LESS SCARY?

You might have some ideas about what could make your fears a little less scary, and a little easier to deal with. Here's an example:

Mary was invited to her friend Sally's birthday party, but she's afraid to meet new people, and she knows there will be new people there. She wants to go to the party, so she comes up with these ideas for making it feel a little less scary to go:

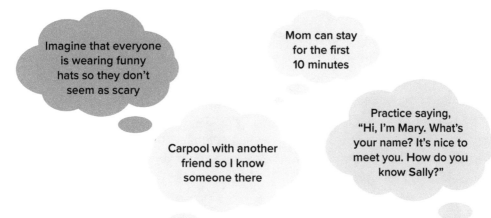

Imagine that everyone is wearing funny hats so they don't seem as scary

Mom can stay for the first 10 minutes

Carpool with another friend so I know someone there

Practice saying, "Hi, I'm Mary. What's your name? It's nice to meet you. How do you know Sally?"

Your turn! What could make your fears a little less scary? Pick one to start with.

My Fear: _____

WHAT IF I'M JUST TOO SCARED TO DO SOMETHING?

I love roller coasters! I remember the first time I went on one, I was so excited that I was finally tall enough to ride it. My family all seemed to be having fun, but I was holding on tight, screaming for help. Like the scared kid in chapter 4 (page 30), I was sure I was going to fall out.

Wait a minute . . . didn't I just say I love roller coasters? How do you think that happened?

If you guessed that I rode the roller coaster again, you're right! If I had never ridden another roller coaster, I would still feel afraid of them, no matter how much I tried to convince myself that they were safe to ride. The more I avoided it, the more scared I would have felt.

If you're like most kids, you probably want to try to stay away from your fears—and the reminders of those fears—as much as possible! This is called "avoidance." When you avoid things, you teach your brain that those things really are scary and dangerous, even if they're not. So the more you avoid them, the more convinced your brain gets that you should be afraid of them.

In times when you do have to face your fears, you don't have to do the scariest thing all at once. You can work your way there by just doing a little bit at a time. Sometimes we feel like we can only handle a little bit and need to avoid feeling all the fear at once, until we build up to it. Remember how I said I love roller coasters now? Well, I took little steps to get braver and braver, like screaming less, then letting go little by little, and eventually I was brave enough to even put my hands in the air. I learned I didn't need to hold on tight to be okay. Then I really started to enjoy roller coasters!

Staying away from the things, and the reminders of things, that you feel scared of can help you feel better—at least *a little* better, right away—for *a little* while. But they can make you feel worse—*a lot* worse—later, and for longer. When you act like your fears and worries are telling you the truth, it actually makes them grow. Plus, the more things you avoid, the more you miss out on, and that's no fun!

So what if you feel too scared to do something? Maybe it feels easier to keep avoiding it. Maybe it's not something that feels that important to you. Maybe you just don't want to feel scared. I wouldn't blame you for not wanting to face that fear!

But what would you be missing out on if you didn't face the fear? What might get better if that fear wasn't bothering you so much anymore? Is there anything that would make it worthwhile?

It's okay to feel scared when you're facing your fears. In fact, one of the most important things about facing your fears is that you can learn that you can handle feeling scared, and that feeling scared doesn't mean something bad will happen. Learning how to handle feeling scared is actually a lot healthier than trying not to feel scared. You can be brave! And remember, you don't have to do the scariest thing all at once.

WHAT ARE MY OBSTACLES?

What do you do to avoid feeling scared? Knowing what things you avoid because you don't want to feel fear or anxiety is important because it helps you make plans for facing your fears. It can help to think of the things you avoid as obstacles to your goal.

Now get out your pencil and think of one fear that's causing problems for you. First, fill in your fear at the start line of the obstacle course, and your goal at the finish line. Then, think of the things that get in the way of that goal—things you try to avoid because of this fear (including any reminders you try to avoid)—and write these on the lines by the obstacles.

WHAT CAN I LEARN FROM FACING MY FEARS?

Now you're going to do an experiment to help you get braver. The experiment will be a test to see if worry is telling you the truth. First, choose one of the obstacles from the obstacle course you just filled out. You might want to choose the thing that sounds easiest, or you might be up for more of a challenge. Either way is okay!

All good experiments start with a plan for what you're going to do and a hypothesis, or guess, about what is going to happen. For this experiment, the hypothesis will be what worry is telling you will happen. Fill in these two boxes with your plan and your hypothesis:

WHAT I'M GOING TO DO TO FACE MY FEAR

WHAT I'M WORRIED WILL HAPPEN

Now it's time to conduct the experiment and evaluate the results. Go ahead and carry out the plan you wrote down to face your fear. When you're done, fill in these three boxes:

WHAT REALLY HAPPENED

WHAT I LEARNED

WHAT I CAN DO TO BE BRAVER NEXT TIME

Great job! Facing your fears is not easy, but reaching your goals is worth it. How do you feel about being able to do that? Keep up the good work! You can use these questions to help you practice getting closer and closer to your goal!

MY FAVORITE PART

In this chapter, you learned:

- Reminders of your fears can "trigger" you to feel scared.

- Acting like your fears are true makes anxiety worse.

- Eventually, finding ways to face your fears makes them feel less scary.

- When you know you can handle feeling scared, you won't need to feel as worried about feeling scared anymore.

You also had the chance to:

- Notice what your reminders (triggers) are.

- Practice coming up with ideas for making your fears a little less scary.

- Figure out what you do to avoid your fears or help you feel safer.

- Do experiments to see what you could learn by facing your fears.

What was your favorite thing you learned or did in this chapter? What did you like about that part?

_____

_____

_____

_____

CHAPTER 6

WHAT CAN I DO TO CALM MY BODY?

Even though it's okay to feel scared, and you even *want* to let yourself feel scared when you practice facing your fears, it can be overwhelming! I'm sure you don't want to be worried or feel scared all the time. In chapter 3, we talked about the fight-flight-freeze alarm system and how it works. In this chapter, we'll talk about what happens to your body when you worry too much, and what you can do to help your body stay healthier and feel better in the face of fear.

WHY DOES MY BODY FEEL DIFFERENT WHEN I WORRY?

Think about how your body feels when you worry. I bet if you really thought about one of your worries right now, you might start to have some of these feelings. Maybe your heart would beat faster or harder. Perhaps you would start to breathe faster or shallower. Your muscles might feel tense, and it might be harder to focus. You might notice other changes as well.

Even if nothing bad or scary is happening when you have worry thoughts, the worry thoughts remind you about things that could happen, so your fight-flight-freeze alarm goes off. You've already learned a lot about why your body reacts in these ways. It's important to know that just thinking about the things that could happen gets your body ready to protect you. These in-the-moment changes can feel uncomfortable, and sometimes scary, but they are not dangerous.

As we talked about in chapter 3, if you feel worried a lot, you might feel tired, like you don't have enough energy. You might have a lot of aches and pains, like headaches, stomachaches, or sore muscles. You probably feel

tense all over a lot of the time, too. You might even breathe a little faster and shallower, and not as slow and deep as a person who is relaxed would. This is because your body is always trying to stay at least a little prepared for possible threats. The alarm doesn't turn off all the way.

It's kind of like if you were walking through a jungle and you knew there were dangerous snakes around. If you saw a snake, or something that looked like a snake, your alarm would go off, and all the in-the-moment changes you've learned about would happen in your body. But when you were just walking and there was no sign of a snake, you would want to stay prepared and on the lookout for any sign of snakes. It would be hard to relax, but you wouldn't be in full-alarm mode, either.

In situations where there's real danger, like the jungle, you probably wouldn't want to relax all the way, because it wouldn't be safe. But most of the things kids worry about aren't the kind of dangers they would need to stay in alert mode for all the time. Instead of helping them, staying in high alert could actually get in the way.

You might be so used to your body being on high alert that you don't even realize these changes are happening in your body, but you might notice that you don't feel well a lot, or don't have as much energy as you want. This can make you feel tired and tense at the same time, which can make it hard to relax (or even sleep, sometimes) and also hard to want to do things. You might also notice that you feel kind of grumpy or get snappy with people. Worrying a lot is no fun! But luckily there are lots of things you can do to help calm your body.

Do you remember when I explained in the last chapter how trying to avoid feeling scared actually makes anxiety worse? It might help you stay out of full-alarm mode, but it keeps you in high-alert mode more of the time, because you feel like you need to stay prepared for possible alarms. When you face your fears and see that you can handle them, it won't feel as scary to think about being in those situations. Then, you won't feel like you need to stay in high-alert mode all the time, and your body can rest. You need to let yourself feel more scared some of the time to feel better the rest of the time.

CHECKING IN WITH MY BODY

You might not always notice the changes that are happening in your body. Doing check-ins, or "scans," to see how your body is feeling will help you know when to use the other tools in this chapter.

Any way your body feels is okay! You don't have to try to change it; instead, you can just notice what is happening for you right now.

Start with your head and "scan down" your body, checking in with each part as you go.

1. Are you squinting your eyes or making wrinkles in your forehead like a frown? Or are your eyes open and forehead smooth? Are you pushing your lips together tightly or clenching your teeth? Or is your tongue at the bottom of your mouth, lips barely touching, teeth apart?

2. Is your body scrunched forward, or straight with your head held high and your shoulders pulled back? Are your shoulders pulled up by your ears or relaxed down?

3. Are you holding your breath, or taking slow, deep breaths?

4. Are you making fists with your hands, or are your fingers straight and loose?

5. Is your belly sucked in tight, or soft and relaxed?

6. Are your legs crossed or folded tight, or straight and relaxed?

7. Are your feet scrunched up with curled toes, or straight and flat?

Great job! How did it feel to do this? Did you notice any changes as you checked in with each part? Try picking three times each day to check in with your body!

LOOKING FOR CLUES: IS IT WORRY?

Since kids sometimes don't realize they're in high-alert mode, sometimes they have to look for other clues. In the last activity, you checked in with your body for tension. In this activity, you'll be looking for other clues in your life that you might be feeling stressed, anxious, or in high-alert mode. Get out a pencil and answer these questions with "yes" or "no."

_____ Have you been having trouble sleeping?

_____ Have you been feeling annoyed by people more than usual?

_____ Do other people seem to be getting upset with you more than usual?

_____ Have you been getting headaches?

_____ Has your stomach been upset a lot?

_____ Do you have less energy than usual?

_____ Have you been getting upset about things more easily than usual?

_____ Have you stopped wanting to do things you used to like?

_____ Has it been harder to remember things?

_____ Have you noticed any other changes in your life?

If you have a lot of "yes" answers, you might be in high-alert mode.

HOW CAN I MAKE MY BODY FEEL BETTER?

Imagine you had a friend who told you they worry a lot of the time. As you talked to them, they shared that they have been feeling tired. Their muscles are sore, and they get a lot of headaches. They stay up late at night, but spend most of their time sitting or lying down, and don't spend much time with friends. What ideas would you have for your friend to help their body feel better?

Now think about yourself. Do you have any ideas for how to make your body feel better? Since you know that staying in high alert is not helping and might be making things worse, you can just relax, right? Okay, go ahead and try it. Ready? 1, 2, 3, relax! Is it working? If you're like most kids, I bet it's not. It would be great if you could just tell yourself, "Relax! It's okay!" and your body would calm down, but it usually doesn't work that way.

Now try to remember a time when you felt really relaxed. Really get into the memory and visualize as many details as you can remember. Did that help? You may have found that this worked a little better to help you feel more relaxed.

Why do you think that is? One reason is that your body needs to learn *how* to relax. Remember, most kids don't even realize how tense their bodies are most of the time, especially if they are used to worrying a lot. Even now that you've started to notice the ways your body changes when it's on high alert, you'll need practice with noticing what it feels like for it to relax. When your mind remembers what it feels like to be relaxed, sometimes it can do a good job of reminding your body.

Do you feel tired a lot? Even though being on high alert puts energy in your muscles to prepare you for action, you might not be getting much exercise You might not feel like doing much, or you might feel like you want to save that energy for if you need it. This means that energy is floating around in your body with nowhere to go. Do you have any ideas about what you can do with this energy?

If you said, "Find ways to use it," you're right! What's the best way to use energy? Exercise! Working your muscles can use up that extra energy so that your body can relax. Getting at least a little exercise every day is a great way to help your body feel better!

What did you notice about your breathing when you did your check-ins? If you noticed it was fast and shallow, like it is for a lot of kids who worry, learning how to take slow, deep breaths can be a helpful tool for relaxing your body.

Do you have trouble sleeping at night? All of these healthy habits will also help you sleep better. Getting enough sleep is important for helping your body (and mind) feel better, too! So make sure to go to bed on time. Most kids your age need between 9 and 11 hours of sleep every day to make their bodies feel the best they can.

Spending time outside in nature and spending time with other people or pets can also help your body relax!

Think about that friend from earlier who worries a lot again. Do you have any more advice to give them now? What about ideas for yourself?

HOW DO I RELAX MY MUSCLES?

Learning to relax your muscles takes practice, just like learning to play a sport or an instrument. This exercise will help you relax your muscles a little at a time. It is a tool to help your body stop being in high-alert mode so much.

Do this exercise one or two times every day, or whenever you feel your body feels like it needs some help relaxing.

1. First, get comfortable. Maybe even lie down. Close your eyes if you'd like.

2. Now pretend you're really angry and trying not to explode. Take a deep breath, make your hands into fists, tighten all the muscles in your arms, and scrunch up your face. Hold your breath and notice how it feels to tense those muscles!

3. Let your breath out and pretend you're suddenly very tired. Let your face muscles get as relaxed as possible, and pretend you're sleeping. Notice how different it feels for those muscles to relax. Do they feel warm and heavy? Take slow, deep breaths and let your muscles get more and more relaxed.

4. Take a deep breath and hold it while you pull your shoulders up to your ears like you're trying to make them hang on your ears like earrings. Pull them up high and notice how it feels to tense those muscles!

5. Now let your breath out and drop your shoulders back down as far from your ears as they'll go. You've decided they don't make good earrings after all! Notice how different it feels for those muscles to relax. Take slow, deep breaths and let your muscles get more and more relaxed.

6. Imagine you have a balloon in your stomach that you're trying to squeeze all the air out of. Pull your stomach in as tight as you can. See if you can pull your belly button in so far it touches your back! Notice how it feels to tense those muscles.

7. Take a breath and let your stomach relax. Notice how different it feels for those muscles to relax. Take slow, deep breaths and let your muscles get more and more relaxed.

8. Without getting up, pretend you want to stand on your tippy-tippy toes using only your legs and feet, but keeping the rest of your body still. Take a deep breath and hold it, then straighten your legs and point your toes. Tense the muscles all the way up your legs and notice how it feels to tense those muscles.

9. Now let your breath go and imagine your legs are so tired that you can't stand. Let all the tension go. Notice how different it feels for those muscles to relax. Do they feel warm and heavy? Take slow, deep breaths and let your whole body get more and more relaxed.

How do you feel now? Do you feel different than you did before?

CALMING BREATH

Taking fast shallow breaths tells your body to stay in high-alert mode. Taking deep, calming breaths tells your body it's okay to relax. Just like learning to relax your muscles, teaching your body to take deep breaths can take practice!

Put one hand on your stomach and the other on your chest and blow out all the air through your mouth. Imagine there's a balloon in your belly and you want to squeeze all of the air out of it. The hand on your belly should go down.

Now, let the air back in through your nose. Imagine you're filling that balloon up. Keep breathing in and filling the balloon in your belly as much as you can! The hand on your belly should go up.

Do this at least 5 more times, squeezing the air out of the balloon by blowing out through your mouth and filling the balloon by breathing in through your nose. Try to breathe out for longer than you breathe in.

How does your body feel now?

MY FAVORITE PART

In this chapter, you learned:

- It's not healthy for your body to be on high alert all the time.

- You can help your body feel better with healthy habits.

- Working your muscles helps your body feel better.

- Learning to take deep breaths and relax your muscles can help your body get out of high-alert mode.

You also had the chance to:

- Notice the changes in your body when you're in high-alert mode.

- Learn and practice how to relax your muscles.

- Learn and practice how to take calming belly breaths.

What was your favorite thing you learned or did in this chapter? What did you like about that part?

_____

_____

_____

_____

_____

CHAPTER 7

WHAT CAN I DO TO CALM MY MIND?

Having a relaxed body can help give a signal to your brain that it doesn't have to stay on high alert. This can sometimes help calm your mind, too. But sometimes your thoughts might stay busy even when your body is calmer. When this happens, it can even make it harder for you to stay calm and relaxed. So it's important to have some tools for calming your mind, too!

In this chapter, you'll learn what a busy mind looks like, what it means to have a calm mind, and how you can calm your mind so you can stay out of high-alert mode.

WHAT DOES IT MEAN TO HAVE A CALM MIND?

Sometimes when I took tests, especially timed ones, I would feel so worried about how I was going to do and how much time was left that it would be hard to focus on the questions, even though I knew the answers. When I saw other kids finish before me, I would get even more worried, and have even more trouble focusing. My mind was too busy!

Can you think of a time when something like this happened to you? Maybe you couldn't find something you needed and were so worried about it being lost that you couldn't see it right in front of you. Maybe you were having trouble understanding questions on your homework and thoughts about how bad you were going to do on it made it harder to focus. Maybe there were a lot of changes happening in your life that seemed to take over your thoughts and made it hard to have fun with your friends. There are a lot of possibilities!

What was happening with your thoughts at that time? Did it feel like they were swirling around in your head like a whirlpool, so fast that it was hard to catch them? Or jumping around like a monkey swinging from branch to branch, never staying in one place? Maybe they were stuck on your worry like a magnet so strong that it was hard to pull them away to focus on anything else?

Chances are, whether you were in full-alarm mode or high-alert mode, your mind was not calm. Some people use the terms "stressed-out" or "overwhelmed" to describe how they feel when their minds are so busy. It can happen when you feel like there's too much going on for you to handle.

When you're under high levels of stress, it can feel like you're walking around in a daze or in a fog, like your mind is somewhere else, and you aren't paying much attention to what's going on around you. You might have trouble thinking of the answers to questions in school, forget things your parents or friends just told you, or lose track of your things because you weren't paying attention to where you put them.

Even if you're looking for something, you might be paying more attention to your thoughts or feelings than what you're looking for. You might also notice that you feel irritated more easily at these times, which can sometimes lead to arguments. These kinds of things can happen a lot when your mind is busy. Luckily, there are things you can do to help yourself feel better! You'll learn about some of these things soon.

If this is what a busy mind looks like, what does it mean to have a calm mind?

A calm mind can focus on one thing at a time, even when there are a lot of other things going on. When your mind is calm, it is aware of what is going on right now (another way of saying this is "being present"). A calm mind can accept what is happening, even if it doesn't like it. Calming your mind takes lots of practice, but it's totally worth it!

PICTURING IT . . . HOW DOES MY MIND FEEL?

Think about a time your mind was busy. In the following picture, draw how your mind feels when it is busy.

Now think about a time your mind was calm. In the following picture, draw how your mind feels when it is calm.

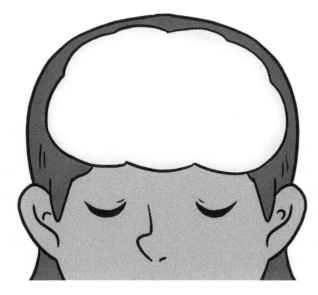

CALM MIND, BUSY MIND . . . WHAT'S DIFFERENT?

The same situation can be way different when your mind is calm than when it is busy.

Think about a situation you've been in sometimes with a busy mind and sometimes with a calm mind. Write the situation on the line at the top.

Then, in the boxes, write or draw about a time your mind was busy when you were in that situation and a time your mind was calm in that same situation. How did things go each time?

Situation: _____

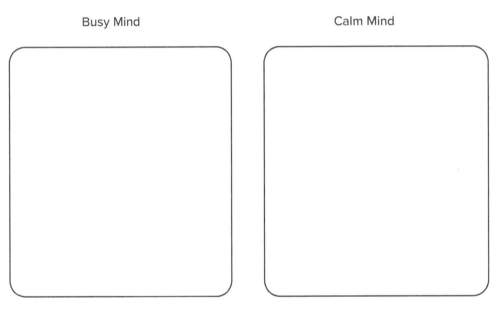

| Busy Mind | Calm Mind |

What was different when your mind was busy? How did it help to have a calm mind?

_____

_____

HOW CAN I CALM MY MIND?

Have you ever heard of mindfulness? Practicing mindfulness is one of the best ways to calm a busy mind. But how does it work?

Before I answer this, stop reading and go get a small snack or a drink. I like to use a piece of chocolate, but you can use whatever you want. Don't eat or drink it yet! Just bring it back and keep reading.

Okay, ready? You're going to use all of your senses to eat or drink what you brought back. Try to be curious about what you'll discover, like an explorer who has never had this snack or drink before and has no idea what to expect.

1. Notice what it looks like: its color, shape, and size.

2. Now smell it.

3. If you move it, does it make any sound?

4. How does it feel in your hand? Is it warm or cold? Heavy or light? Smooth or rough?

You're finally ready to taste it! Take a sip or a bite, but don't swallow yet! Try to keep it in your mouth a little longer than you usually would so you can really pay attention to it. How does it feel in your mouth? Can you hear it? Smell it? How does it taste? When you swallow, see if you can feel it go all the way down into your stomach.

Were you able to do it? Congratulations! You just practiced being mindful. You can be mindful of anything—your breathing, what you're doing, what you're thinking, how you're feeling, or what's going on around you. All you have to do is to decide to pay attention to it, be okay with whatever you notice, and bring your attention back when it wanders away. Mindfulness is about being present in the moment and aware of what's happening right now instead of thinking about what happened in the past or what could happen in the future.

Some people feel frustrated when their mind wanders a lot, and they think that means they're bad at mindfulness. But everyone's mind wanders sometimes! Your mind will probably wander a lot when you first start practicing.

Some days it might be easier to keep your attention where you want it, and some days it might be harder. That's normal. The goal of mindfulness is not to stop thinking. The goal is to change how your thoughts affect you. Just noticing when your mind wanders is being mindful. The more you practice, the easier it will get!

Being able to focus on what's happening right now, one thing at a time, without getting upset about it, can help calm a busy mind. It's like putting an anchor down in a stormy sea of thoughts (or that whirlpool) to keep you in one place. It doesn't stop the storm of other thoughts from happening, but it keeps them from tossing you all over the place. It can help train the swinging monkey in your thoughts to keep coming back to the branch you want it on before it wanders too far for too long. And it can help weaken the magnet of your worry thoughts that try to pull you away from what's happening now, so you can be more present.

When you're able to do this mindfulness practice, it can help you get out of high-alert mode and feel less anxious or overwhelmed. It can help you pause and make better choices about how to respond when you're feeling

stressed. Best of all, when you're able to focus on enjoying what's actually happening (instead of what worry is telling you *could* happen) you'll be able to have a lot more fun! What are some ways or times mindfulness could be helpful for you?

SETTING ASIDE WORRIES FOR LATER

You've learned about how it's important to understand your worries and not try to avoid them. It's also important not to pay so much attention to them that they take over your life!

Setting your worries aside for later is a way to use mindfulness to do both of these things. Pick a time to spend 10 to 20 minutes focusing on your worries every day. Make sure it's a time when you can do something else after, so not right before bed.

During this time, use your mindfulness tools to pay attention to your worry thoughts and feelings. You can write your worries down, tell them to someone else, or just think about them during this time. Set a timer so you know when you're done.

When you're done, use your mindfulness skills to set your worries aside for later and pay attention to whatever else you're doing. If you have a worry thought, imagine setting it on an imaginary shelf (or drawer or box) until the next time you have scheduled to worry.

The worry might come back a lot at first, and that's okay. Don't push it away. Instead, just set it aside and tell it, "I know you're there. I'm doing something else right now. I'll pay attention to you later."

Now make a plan!

1. The time of day I will spend focusing on worries is _____.

2. I will focus on my worries for _____ minutes.

3. I will focus on my worries by (circle one): writing, telling someone else, thinking about them.

4. The rest of the time, I will set my worries aside in/on an imaginary

   _____.

5. When worries come back, I will _____.

MINDFULNESS TOUR

This mindfulness tour will give you a chance to practice being mindful using all your senses. Stay at each stop as long as you want, but take at least a few breaths at each.

See how many things you can notice that you weren't paying attention to and take some "mental pictures" along the way!

STOP #1. **Sight:** Notice what you can see. You can look for things that are a certain shape or color, or just see if there's anything you haven't noticed before.

STOP #2. **Hearing:** Notice what sounds are going on around you. See if you can focus on one sound at a time.

STOP #3. **Smell and Taste:** See if there's anything you can smell or taste (even if you aren't eating).

STOP #4. **Touch:** Notice the temperatures and textures of your clothes and whatever you're sitting on. Try walking and see how the ground feels under your feet, then sit back down.

STOP #5. **Sensations:** Focus on the sensations inside your body. Is anything tense? Does anything hurt? What emotions are you having?

STOP #6. **Breath:** Count 10 of your breaths. Notice how it feels for the air to go in and out.

STOP #7. **Thoughts:** What kinds of thoughts are you having? Are they moving fast or slow? Just notice each thought and then move to the next.

What was your favorite part? Remember, you can visit any of the stops on this tour, or even take the whole tour again, anytime you want to help calm your mind!

MY FAVORITE PART

In this chapter, you learned:

- The difference between a calm mind and a busy mind.

- The kinds of problems that can happen when your mind is busy.

- What mindfulness is.

- How to use mindfulness to calm your busy mind.

- The ways that having a calm mind can help you.

You also had the chance to:

- Notice what your mind feels like when it is calm and when it is busy.

- Think about how situations go differently when your mind is busy or calm.

- Practice many different ways of being mindful.

What was your favorite thing you learned or did in this chapter? What did you like about that part?

_____

_____

_____

_____

_____

★ **CHAPTER 8** ★

WHAT IF MY WORRIES COME BACK?

If you've been doing the activities in this book, you might notice that you're starting to feel better. Maybe some of your worries have gone away or don't bother you as much as they used to. Hopefully you feel a little more confident that you can handle anxious feelings when they happen and that you don't have to feel afraid of anxiety or worry anymore. You've done a great job!

But what if those worries come back, or start to bother you more again? And what do you do with the worries that haven't gotten better yet? In this chapter, you will learn how to keep using all the skills you've learned in this book to help you continue to feel better now, and when your worries come back.

WILL MY WORRIES GO AWAY?

You might still be having worries and wonder if they'll ever go away. Or if your worries are gone, you might be wondering if they'll come back. These are great questions! Most kids who worry a lot hope to get rid of their worries forever.

Can you think of any times in your life when you've had worries that have gone away and come back? Or times you've felt less worried, and then a new worry started? Maybe you even thought you were done worrying forever, but then started to worry again. I know this has happened lots of times for me!

It's normal for worries to go away for a while and then come back. You might be wondering, "Why?"

When you use the tools in this book, you create new thoughts and memories about worry that feel better than the old ones, but the old thoughts and memories don't completely go away. Imagine that your worry thoughts were a painting. The tools in this book help you paint a new picture over the old one, but the old one is still there underneath. Sometimes the new paint fades or gets wiped away, and the old picture starts to come through again, so you need to touch up the paint on the new picture.

There are a lot of things that can make your old worries come back. For example, if you're worried about getting shots at the doctor's office and then do some brave activities to help you be able to get a shot, you might stop worrying about shots for a while. But if you don't need to get another shot for a long time, your fear of shots might come back because you're out of practice.

Or if you had stopped being worried about shots and then got a shot that hurt a lot after having a bunch of shots that weren't so bad, or got sick and had to have a lot of shots, that could also bring back your worry about getting shots.

Feeling stressed or overwhelmed can also make worries come back. This can happen when there are big changes happening in your life, or when you're tired or have a lot going on. If you just moved to a new town and started at a new school, you might feel more worried about going to get a shot than if you had to get a shot before going on a vacation that you were excited about.

Most kids feel upset when their worries come back, especially if they thought they were gone forever. Sometimes even thinking about their worries coming back makes them feel bad about themselves. But starting to worry again doesn't mean anything bad about you!

Don't forget that worries can also be helpful! They can help protect you, as well as show good things about the kind of person you are and what's important to you. Sometimes worries come back to remind you of those things, like a signal. Even though it sounds nice, it probably wouldn't be a good thing for you to never worry again. The important thing is to be prepared!

PREPARING MY THOUGHTS

It can be hard when worries come back. One step to being prepared for worries coming back is to be ready for the things you might tell yourself about those worries. Sometimes kids think things like, "Those tools I learned didn't really help," or "I'll never really feel better," even if they really did feel better when they used the tools. They might even think that worries coming back means there's something wrong with them.

You know now that it's normal for worries to come back sometimes, but it can be easy to forget these things when worries start again. Luckily, you've also learned how to talk back to exaggerated thoughts. When you are ready for these thoughts, you can have a plan for what to say back to them.

What negative thoughts do you think you might have if your worries came back?

_____

_____

_____

_____

_____

What can you tell yourself if your worries come back? What thoughts do you think would be helpful?

_____

_____

_____

_____

_____

KNOWING MY SIGNS AND SITUATIONS

Another great way to prepare for when worries come back is to know what signs to look for. Are there things you start to avoid? Are there things you start to do? Do you start having headaches or stomachaches? What are some situations you might want to be prepared to use your worry tools in? Are there certain reminders you know are likely to bring your worries back?

Write your signs and situations on the following signs. Some examples might be "trouble sleeping," "wanting to avoid school," or "meeting new people."

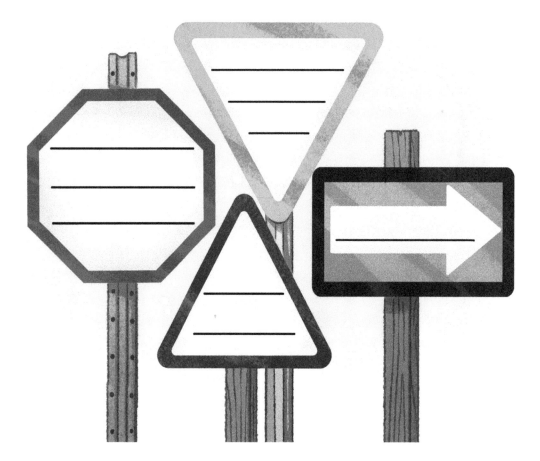

WHAT CAN I DO IF MY WORRIES COME BACK?

Imagine that you lifted a weight as many times as you could every day. What do you think would happen over time? You'd probably get stronger, right? And you would probably be able to lift that same weight more and more times. Even if the weight had felt really heavy and hard to lift at first, it might start to feel lighter and easier to lift as you got stronger.

Now imagine that you decided you were strong enough and didn't need to keep lifting the weight anymore, so you stopped doing it. If you went to lift the weight again in a few months or a year, do you think you would still be able to lift it as many times as you could when you stopped? Probably not, right?

It might feel frustrating when you couldn't lift the weight as easily. But would it mean that you were weak or not capable of doing it anymore? Of course not! It would just mean you were out of practice.

So what would you need to do to get better at lifting the weight again? That's right! You'd need to start lifting it again, and your strength would build over time, just like it did the first time.

The same is true for your worries and the skills you've learned in this book. When worries come back, it doesn't mean anything bad about kids or the work they did to feel better. Most of the time, when worries come back, it's because kids have stopped using their skills. Just like lifting that weight, the solution is to start using your skills again.

Start with the tools that worked best for you the first time. In a little bit, you'll be making a tool kit of all the skills you've learned. You can use that to remind yourself of what to do when your worries come back. You can also read through this book and do the activities again if you need an extra reminder or a little more help.

Think about the worry painting with the new painting over it. Would it be easier to touch up the new painting when you first notice it fading, or after it's mostly faded away? I bet your answer is "the sooner, the better!"

The faster you catch your worries when they start to come back, the easier it will be to use the skills you've learned, and the faster you'll feel better. When kids wait a long time before they start to use their tools again, their worries have more time to build.

The solution is to start using your skills again as soon as you notice your worries are starting to come back. That's why it's important to know what the signs are that your worries are coming back, and have a plan for what you can do when they do. With a little planning, you can stop worries in their tracks!

What if you don't catch the worries right away? It's okay! Even if you forget to use your skills until your worries get worse and start to get in the way again, the tools you learned will still work, but it might just take a little extra effort. But you did it once, and I know you can do it again!

WHAT WOULD I TELL A FRIEND?

Imagine you had a friend named Jane. One day, Jane came to you and said:

"I'm feeling really upset lately. I feel worried all the time, and it's making it hard to pay attention in school. I don't want to go anywhere, because I'm worried about what will happen when I'm out. I've even been getting into fights with my parents about it. I feel like there's something wrong with me, and I don't think anyone understands!"

What advice would you give Jane? What could you say to help Jane feel better?

_____

_____

_____

_____

_____

WORRY SKILLS TOOL KIT

You've learned a lot of new tools in this book. You've also had the chance to practice these skills. You've worked hard! How does it feel?

Most kids find some favorite tools that work best for them. Write your favorite tools in this tool kit to help you remember them when your worries come back. It might help to flip back through the exercises in this book to jog your memory.

Pull out your tool kit any time you start to notice signs that your worry is coming back. It can also help to remind yourself of these tools when you are going into a situation where you think there's a good chance you will feel anxious.

Remember that you have the tools and you know how to use them. You can do it!

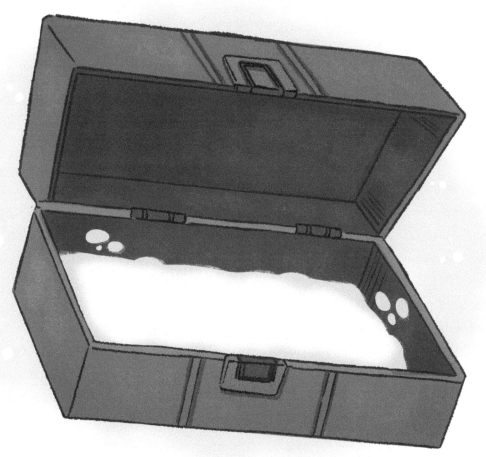

MY FAVORITE PART

In this chapter, you learned:

- How to prepare for worries coming back.

- That using the skills in this book will help again, just like they helped the first time.

- That the faster you catch your worries coming back and start using the tools again, the faster you'll feel better again!

You also had the chance to:

- Think about how to use your tools in different situations.

- Prepare your thoughts for worry coming back.

- Create your own worry skills tool kit.

What was your favorite thing you learned or did in this chapter? What did you like about that part?

_____

_____

_____

_____

_____

CHAPTER 9

I'VE GOT THIS!

Think about a time when you went on a trip or had an adventure. What did you do after it ended? Did you look at pictures? Did you think about the things you did, or maybe tell someone else about it? Doing these kinds of things at the end of a journey helps make memories stronger, which helps you remember them better and for longer.

Now you are nearing the end of your adventure with this book. Your journey isn't over, and it might never be, because worry is a part of life for everyone. But you are ready to move on to the next step.

Maybe you've gotten really good at using the tools you've learned, and you're ready to go out on your own and use them. Maybe you want to go back and work on some of the parts of this book again. Or maybe you're ready to learn even more tools from other places (there are some ideas for where you can get these later in the book on page 87).

Before moving on to that next step, it's time to think about your journey so far, to help you remember what you've learned and what you've accomplished!

Even if you still feel worried a lot, chances are you've come a long way from where you started. It's important to see what progress you've made. This can help you feel more confident that you can handle worries now and in the future.

I'm proud of you, and I hope you feel proud of yourself! The more you use the tools you've learned in this book, the easier it will get. Keep up the great work, and I'm sure you'll be an expert at handling worries!

WHAT'S BETTER WITH LESS WORRY?

One thing that has probably changed for you after working through this book is how you feel about your worries. You might still have worries, but now that they don't bother you as much, they don't get in the way as much. This means you can do more and enjoy life more!

Get out a pencil or something colorful to draw with and write or draw about all the things you can do in your life now that worry doesn't bother you so much. What can you do? What can you enjoy more? What are some things you still want to work toward as you get better and better at handling worry?

MY WORRY ADVENTURE

Writing down your story from start to end is a great way to help you remember what you've learned. Get out a pencil and fill in the blanks with your answers.

Before I read this book, I felt _____ *a lot.*

Feeling that way caused some problems, like _____ ,

_____ ,

and _____ . *I thought* _____ .

These thoughts and problems made me feel _____ .

I've learned a lot since then. Some of the things I learned are _____

_____ , _____ , *and* _____ . *I have a*

lot of tools for handling worry and anxiety now, too! Some of my favorite

tools are _____ , _____ ,

and _____ . *These help me* _____ .

Now I know _____ . *I can* _____ . *And*

that feels _____ !

MY FAVORITE PART

In this book you've learned:

- That worry exaggerates and causes false alarms.

- That the way your body feels when you are anxious is caused by the fight-flight-freeze response that everybody has.

- That your thoughts, feelings, and actions are all connected.

- That you can handle worry and anxiety, and that you don't need to be afraid of them!

You've also had a chance to practice:

- Noticing when and how worry is exaggerating how bad things are.

- Facing your fears.

- Talking back to your worries.

- Many different ways of relaxing and being mindful.

You've learned and practiced a lot! Learning to handle worry can be hard work, but it can also be fun and interesting! Now you have a whole tool kit full of skills for what to do when you worry.

What was your favorite thing you learned or did in this book? What did you like about that part?

_____

_____

_____

_____

What are some things you're proud of?

_____

_____

_____

What are some things you're feeling hopeful about?

_____

_____

_____

MORE FOR KIDS

Now that you've finished all the activities in this book, you might be ready for even more activities to try! Here are some websites and apps with more activities to help you practice the tools you learned. (Make sure you check with your grown-ups before you use any of these apps or websites.)

Mindfulness Meditation Tools

Headspace
Headspace.com/meditation/kids
This is a website and an app with meditations made for kids. There are meditations for anxiety, focus, sleep, and other things. You can try it out for free.

Insight Timer
InsightTimer.com/meditation-topics/kids-meditation
This website has tons of free meditations for kids. There's an app, too!

CBT Tools for Anxiety

Gozen.com
This is a program with videos for helping kids with worry and anxiety. There's a book, too. This costs money, so make sure to ask your parents!

Manatee & Me
GetManatee.com
Earn points for using your skills with this app!

Positive Penguins
PositivePenguins.com
This is an app that will help you catch and challenge your negative thinking. It will also help you see how your thoughts and feelings are connected. It was even designed by a kid!

MORE FOR PARENTS AND CAREGIVERS

. . . .

Organizations

Anxiety and Depression Association of America: ADAA.org/finding-help /children

The Child Anxiety Network: ChildAnxiety.net

Child Mind Institute: ChildMind.org/topics/concerns/anxiety

WorryWise Kids: WorryWiseKids.org

Books

Anxiety Relief for Kids: On-the-Spot Strategies to Help Your Child Overcome Worry, Panic, and Avoidance by Bridget Flynn Walker, PhD

Breaking Free of Child Anxiety and OCD: A Scientifically Proven Program for Parents by Eli R. Lebowitz, PhD

Freeing Your Child from Anxiety: Powerful, Practical Solutions to Overcome Your Child's Fears, Worries, and Phobias by Tamar E. Chansky

Helping Your Anxious Child: A Step-by-Step Guide for Parents by Ronald Rapee, PhD; Ann Wignall, PsyD; Susan Spence, PhD; Heidi Lyneham, PhD; and Vanessa Cobham, PhD

Websites

AT Parenting Survival
AnxiousToddlers.com

Big Life Journal
BigLifeJournal.com

Coping Cat Parents
CopingCatParents.com

REFERENCES

Burns, David D. *Ten Days to Self-Esteem*. New York: Quill, 1993.

Burns, David D. *When Panic Attacks: the New, Drug-Free Anxiety Therapy That Can Change Your Life*. New York: Morgan Road Books, 2006.

Ciarrochi, Joseph, Louise Hayes, and Ann Bailey. *Get Out of Your Mind & Into Your Life for Teens: A Guide to Living an Extraordinary Life*. Oakland, CA: Instant Help Books, 2012.

Craske, Michelle G., Michael Treanor, Chris Conway, Tomislav Zbozinek, and Bram Vervliet. "Maximizing Exposure Therapy: An Inhibitory Learning Approach." *Behaviour Research and Therapy* 58 (July 2014): 10–23. ncbi.nlm .nih .gov/pmc/articles/PMC4114726/#_ffn_sectitle.

Lebowitz, Eli R., and Haim Omer. *Treating Childhood and Adolescent Anxiety: A Guide for Caregivers*. Hoboken, NJ: John Wiley & Sons, 2013.

Siegel, Daniel J., and Tina Payne Bryson. *The Whole-Brain Child*. New York: Bantam Books, 2012.

INDEX